IRELAND

Photographs by Tom Kelly

&

Address Book

Pomegranate

San Francisco

03/23

$1.00

Published by Pomegranate
Box 6099, Rohnert Park, California 94927

Pomegranate Europe Ltd.
Fullbridge House, Fullbridge
Maldon, Essex CM9 4LE, England

© 1997 Tom Kelly

All rights reserved.
No part of this book may be reproduced or transmitted in any form
or by any means, electronic or mechanical, including photocopying,
recording, or by any information storage and retrieval system,
without permission in writing from the copyright holders.

ISBN 0-7649-0380-2
Catalog No. A917

Tom Kelly's photographs are featured in annual calendars and a book
of postcards published by Pomegranate. He has also had several books
published, three with Roberts Rinehart Publishers in Boulder, Colorado.

Cover photograph: Cliffs of Moher, County Clare

Back cover photograph: County Donegal

Title page: Cooley, County Louth

Designed by Shannon Lemme

Printed in Hong Kong

05 04 03 02 01 00 99 98   10 9 8 7 6 5 4 3 2
First Edition

Considered internationally as Ireland's greatest photographer, Tom Kelly was born in Limerick, Ireland, in 1952 and has worked all over the world as a free-lance photographer and graphics designer. His photographs reveal an Irish landscape in flux between the misty land of shifting light and soft colors, and a place where economic realities are evident in the contours of the land. Kelly's books include *Ireland: The Living Landscape* (Roberts Rinehart, 1992), with poetry by Seamus Heaney; *Legendary Ireland* (Roberts Rinehart, 1995); *Literary Ireland* (Roberts Rinehart, 1997); *The Insight Guide to Ireland*; *The AA Guide to Ireland*; and *Reader's Digest Ireland*.

Tom Kelly's photographs have also been published in major magazines such as *Vogue*, *Geo*, and *Country Living*, as well as Pomegranate's *Ireland* calendars (wall and engagement) and *Ireland: A Book of Postcards*. He currently lives in Dublin.

County Kerry

Welcome Earth,
My natural heritage! and this soft turf,
These rocks, which no insidious ocean saps,
But the wise air flows over, and the sun
Illumines.

—Edward Dowden (1843–1913)
On the Heights

Bray Head, County Wicklow

'Twas a balmy summer morning,
Warm and early,
Such as only June bestows;
Everywhere the earth adorning...
—James Clarence Mangan (1803–1849)
The Dawning of the Day

NAME

PHONE

ADDRESS

FAX

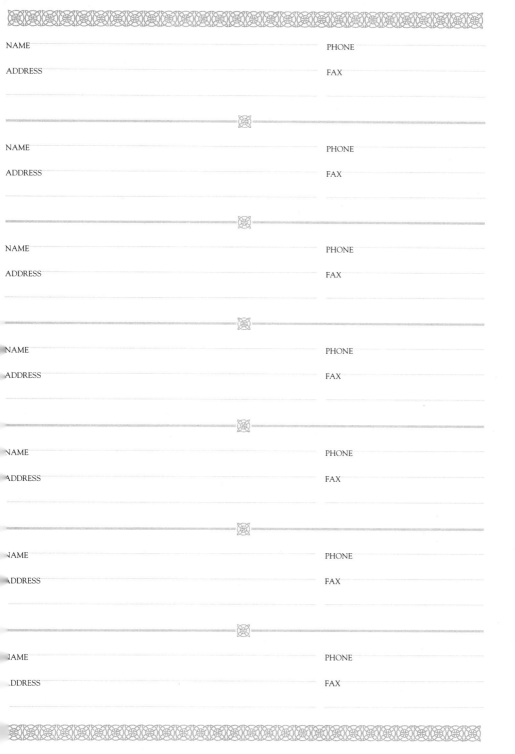

NAME

PHONE

ADDRESS

FAX

NAME

PHONE

ADDRESS

FAX

NAME

PHONE

ADDRESS

FAX

NAME

PHONE

ADDRESS

FAX

NAME

PHONE

ADDRESS

FAX

NAME

PHONE

ADDRESS

FAX

NAME _____ PHONE _____

ADDRESS _____ FAX _____

_____ _____

NAME _____ PHONE _____

ADDRESS _____ FAX _____

_____ _____

NAME _____ PHONE _____

ADDRESS _____ FAX _____

_____ _____

NAME _____ PHONE _____

ADDRESS _____ FAX _____

_____ _____

NAME _____ PHONE _____

ADDRESS _____ FAX _____

_____ _____

NAME _____ PHONE _____

ADDRESS _____ FAX _____

_____ _____

NAME _____ PHONE _____

ADDRESS _____ FAX _____

NAME   PHONE

ADDRESS   FAX

NAME   PHONE

ADDRESS   FAX

NAME   PHONE

ADDRESS   FAX

NAME   PHONE

ADDRESS   FAX

NAME   PHONE

ADDRESS   FAX

NAME   PHONE

ADDRESS   FAX

NAME   PHONE

ADDRESS   FAX

NAME   PHONE

ADDRESS   FAX

NAME   PHONE

ADDRESS   FAX

NAME   PHONE

ADDRESS   FAX

NAME   PHONE

ADDRESS   FAX

NAME   PHONE

ADDRESS   FAX

NAME   PHONE

ADDRESS   FAX

NAME   PHONE

ADDRESS   FAX

Cooley, County Louth

I know a valley fair,
Eileen aroon!
I knew a cottage there,
Eileen aroon!

—Gerald Griffin (1803–1840)
Eileen Aroon (Eileen, my treasure)

B

Doolough, Delphi, County Mayo

Were it not that full of sorrow from my people forth I go,
By the blessed sun, 'tis royally I'd sing thy praise, Mayo.
—George Fox (1624–1691)
The County of Mayo

NAME

PHONE

ADDRESS

FAX

NAME

Tom & Kim Bongi
Home: (925) 362-0610
E-Mail: Bongotk@aol.com
300 Hartfield Rd
Danville, CA 94526

NE

ADDRESS

NAME

PHONE

ADDRESS

FAX

NAME

PHONE

ADDRESS

FAX

NAME

PHONE

ADDRESS

FAX

NAME

PHONE

ADDRESS

FAX

NAME

PHONE

ADDRESS

FAX

NAME

ADDRESS

PHONE

FAX

NAME

ADDRESS

PHONE

FAX

NAME

ADDRESS

PHONE

FAX

NAME

ADDRESS

PHONE

FAX

NAME

ADDRESS

PHONE

FAX

NAME

ADDRESS

PHONE

FAX

NAME

ADDRESS

PHONE

FAX

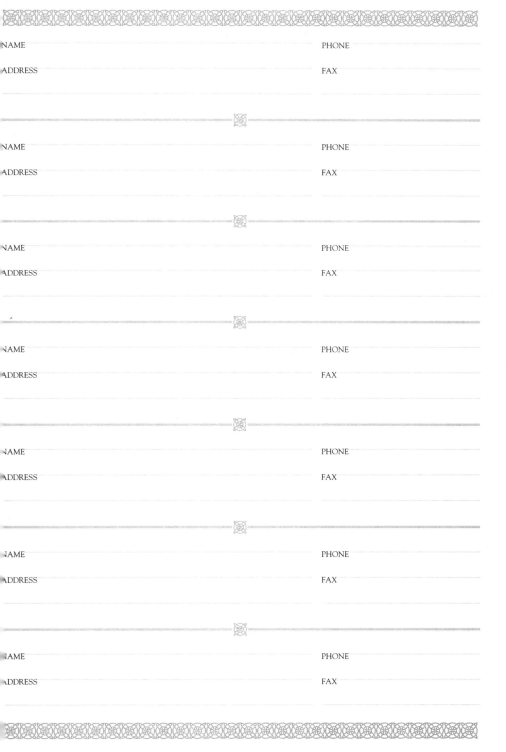

NAME

PHONE

ADDRESS

FAX

NAME

PHONE

ADDRESS

FAX

NAME

PHONE

ADDRESS

FAX

NAME

PHONE

ADDRESS

FAX

NAME

PHONE

ADDRESS

FAX

NAME

PHONE

ADDRESS

FAX

NAME

PHONE

ADDRESS

FAX

NAME _____

PHONE _____

ADDRESS _____

FAX _____

_____

_____

NAME _____

PHONE _____

ADDRESS _____

FAX _____

_____

_____

NAME _____

PHONE _____

ADDRESS _____

FAX _____

_____

_____

NAME _____

PHONE _____

ADDRESS _____

FAX _____

_____

_____

NAME _____

PHONE _____

ADDRESS _____

FAX _____

_____

_____

NAME _____

PHONE _____

ADDRESS _____

FAX _____

_____

_____

NAME _____

PHONE _____

ADDRESS _____

FAX _____

_____

Baltinglass, County Wicklow

The massive capes and ruined towers seem conscious
of the calm....

—Thomas Davis (1814–1845)
The Sack of Baltimore

C

Ros Beg, County Donegal

In short, it was a most delicious morn—
What clouds there were soared in the upper sky,
Or round the mountains died as they were born
In the bright haze that cling mysteriously
To the dim coast.

—John Todhunter (1839–1916)
Morning in the Bay of Naples

NAME

ADDRESS

Al&Dot Crosby   NE
Home: (602) 743-0667
E-Mail: acndc@azstarnet.com
3333 N 6th Bar Spur
Tucson, AZ 85745

NAME   PHONE

ADDRESS   FAX

NAME   PHONE

ADDRESS   FAX

NAME   PHONE

ADDRESS   FAX

NAME   PHONE

ADDRESS   FAX

AME   PHONE

DDRESS   FAX

AME   PHONE

DDRESS   FAX

NAME _____ PHONE _____

ADDRESS _____ FAX _____

_____

————————————————— ⬚ —————————————————

NAME _____ PHONE _____

ADDRESS _____ FAX _____

_____

————————————————— ⬚ —————————————————

NAME _____ PHONE _____

ADDRESS _____ FAX _____

_____

————————————————— ⬚ —————————————————

NAME _____ PHONE _____

ADDRESS _____ FAX _____

_____

————————————————— ⬚ —————————————————

NAME _____ PHONE _____

ADDRESS _____ FAX _____

_____

————————————————— ⬚ —————————————————

NAME _____ PHONE _____

ADDRESS _____ FAX _____

_____

————————————————— ⬚ —————————————————

NAME _____ PHONE _____

ADDRESS _____ FAX _____

_____

NAME   PHONE

ADDRESS   FAX

NAME   PHONE

ADDRESS   FAX

NAME   PHONE

ADDRESS   FAX

NAME   PHONE

ADDRESS   FAX

NAME   PHONE

ADDRESS   FAX

NAME   PHONE

ADDRESS   FAX

NAME   PHONE

ADDRESS   FAX

NAME

ADDRESS

PHONE

FAX

NAME

ADDRESS

PHONE

FAX

NAME

ADDRESS

PHONE

FAX

NAME

ADDRESS

PHONE

FAX

NAME

ADDRESS

PHONE

FAX

NAME

ADDRESS

PHONE

FAX

NAME

ADDRESS

PHONE

FAX

Glenmalure, County Wicklow

Once more, through God's high will, and grace
Of hours that each its task fulfills,
Heart-healing Spring resumes her place,
The valley throngs, and scales the hills.
—Sir Aubrey de Vere (1788–1846)
The Year of Sorrow 1849, Spring

D

Tory Island, County Donegal

Sing, *Gile machree*,
Sit down by me,
We now are joined and ne'er shall sever;
This hearth's our own,
Our hearts are one,
And peace is ours for ever!

—Gerald Griffin (1803–1840)
Gile Machree

NAME	~~ONE~~ PHONE
Brendan Daly	
	Home: (503) 235-7166
ADDRESS	**E-Mail:** brendan_daly@hotmail.com
	3033 SE 26th
	Portland, OR 97202

NAME	~~ONE~~ PHONE
Colin Daly	
	Home: (415) 642-5869
ADDRESS	**E-Mail:** colin_daly@mailcity.com
	2933 Folsom
	San Franciscg, CA 94119

NAME	PHONE
ADDRESS	FAX

NAME	PHONE
ADDRESS	FAX

NAME	PHONE
ADDRESS	FAX

NAME	PHONE
ADDRESS	FAX

NAME	PHONE
ADDRESS	FAX

NAME

ADDRESS

PHONE

FAX

NAME

ADDRESS

PHONE

FAX

NAME

ADDRESS

PHONE

FAX

NAME

ADDRESS

PHONE

FAX

NAME

ADDRESS

PHONE

FAX

NAME

ADDRESS

PHONE

FAX

NAME

ADDRESS

PHONE

FAX

NAME

PHONE

ADDRESS

FAX

NAME

PHONE

ADDRESS

FAX

NAME

PHONE

ADDRESS

FAX

NAME

PHONE

ADDRESS

FAX

NAME

PHONE

ADDRESS

FAX

NAME

PHONE

ADDRESS

FAX

NAME

PHONE

ADDRESS

FAX

NAME _____ PHONE _____

ADDRESS _____ FAX _____

_____

NAME _____ PHONE _____

ADDRESS _____ FAX _____

_____

NAME _____ PHONE _____

ADDRESS _____ FAX _____

_____

NAME _____ PHONE _____

ADDRESS _____ FAX _____

_____

NAME _____ PHONE _____

ADDRESS _____ FAX _____

_____

NAME _____ PHONE _____

ADDRESS _____ FAX _____

_____

NAME _____ PHONE _____

ADDRESS _____ FAX _____

_____

County Donegal

O, I long, I am pining again to behold
The land that belongs to the brave Gael of old;
Far dearer to my heart than a gift of gems or gold
Are the fair Hills of Eire, O!
—James Clarence Mangan (1803–1845),
translated from the Gaelic
The Fair Hills of Eire, O!

Delphi, County Mayo

So simple is the earth we tread,
So quick with love and life her frame,
Ten thousand years have dawned and fled,
And still her magic is the same.
—Stopford A. Brooke (1832–1916)
The Earth and Man

NAME   PHONE

Antone & Nancy Eppolito
19 Ely Drive
Fayetteville, New York 13066

ADDRESS

NAME   PHONE

ADDRESS   FAX

NAME   PHONE

ADDRESS   FAX

NAME   PHONE

ADDRESS   FAX

NAME   PHONE

ADDRESS   FAX

NAME   PHONE

ADDRESS   FAX

NAME   PHONE

ADDRESS   FAX

NAME   PHONE

ADDRESS   FAX

NAME   PHONE

ADDRESS   FAX

NAME   PHONE

ADDRESS   FAX

NAME   PHONE

ADDRESS   FAX

NAME   PHONE

ADDRESS   FAX

NAME   PHONE

ADDRESS   FAX

NAME   PHONE

ADDRESS   FAX

NAME   PHONE

ADDRESS   FAX

NAME   PHONE

ADDRESS   FAX

NAME   PHONE

ADDRESS   FAX

NAME   PHONE

ADDRESS   FAX

NAME   PHONE

ADDRESS   FAX

NAME   PHONE

ADDRESS   FAX

NAME   PHONE

ADDRESS   FAX

NAME

PHONE

ADDRESS

FAX

NAME

PHONE

ADDRESS

FAX

NAME

PHONE

ADDRESS

FAX

NAME

PHONE

ADDRESS

FAX

NAME

PHONE

ADDRESS

FAX

NAME

PHONE

ADDRESS

FAX

NAME

PHONE

ADDRESS

FAX

Louisburg, County Mayo

Now with the coming in of the spring the days will stretch a bit,
And after the Feast of Brigid I shall hoist my flag and go,
For since the thought got into my head I can neither stand nor sit
Until I find myself in the middle of the County of Mayo.
—James Stephens (1882–1950)
The County Mayo

G

Tor Mor, County Cork

They are going, going, going from the valleys and the hills,
They are leaving far behind them heathery moor and mountain rills,
All the wealth of hawthorn hedges where the brown thrush sways and trills.
—Mrs. Seumas MacManus (Ethna Carbery) (1866–1902)
The Passing of the Gael

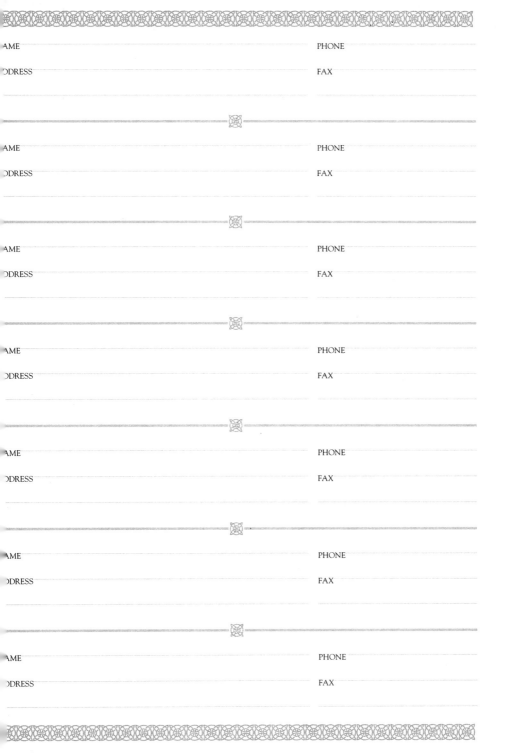

NAME

PHONE

ADDRESS

FAX

NAME

PHONE

ADDRESS

FAX

NAME

PHONE

ADDRESS

FAX

NAME

PHONE

ADDRESS

FAX

NAME

PHONE

ADDRESS

FAX

NAME

PHONE

ADDRESS

FAX

NAME

PHONE

ADDRESS

FAX

NAME   PHONE

ADDRESS   FAX

NAME   PHONE

ADDRESS   FAX

NAME   PHONE

ADDRESS   FAX

NAME   PHONE

ADDRESS   FAX

NAME   PHONE

ADDRESS   FAX

NAME   PHONE

ADDRESS   FAX

NAME   PHONE

ADDRESS   FAX

NAME _____ PHONE _____

ADDRESS _____ FAX _____

_____ _____

NAME _____ PHONE _____

ADDRESS _____ FAX _____

_____ _____

NAME _____ PHONE _____

ADDRESS _____ FAX _____

_____ _____

NAME _____ PHONE _____

ADDRESS _____ FAX _____

_____ _____

NAME _____ PHONE _____

ADDRESS _____ FAX _____

_____ _____

NAME _____ PHONE _____

ADDRESS _____ FAX _____

_____ _____

NAME _____ PHONE _____

ADDRESS _____ FAX _____

_____ _____

NAME _____ PHONE _____

ADDRESS _____ FAX _____

_____

NAME _____ PHONE _____

ADDRESS _____ FAX _____

_____

NAME _____ PHONE _____

ADDRESS _____ FAX _____

_____

NAME _____ PHONE _____

ADDRESS _____ FAX _____

_____

NAME _____ PHONE _____

ADDRESS _____ FAX _____

_____

NAME _____ PHONE _____

ADDRESS _____ FAX _____

_____

NAME _____ PHONE _____

ADDRESS _____ FAX _____

Cahir Castle, County Tipperary

Ah! well-a day, the mists of age
May make these summer seasons dim;
No matter—still in Chaucer's page
The olden summers shine for him.
—Thomas Caulfield Irwin (1823–1892)
A Character

Lough Ree, Longford, County Meath

There is not in the wide world a valley so sweet
As that vale in whose bosom the bright waters meet;
O the last rays of feeling and life must depart,
Ere the bloom of that valley shall fade from my heart.
—Thomas Moore (1780–1852)
The Meeting of the Waters

AME _____ PHONE _____

DDRESS _____ FAX _____

_____

AME _____ PHONE _____

DDRESS _____ FAX _____

_____

AME _____ PHONE _____

DDRESS _____ FAX _____

_____

AME _____ PHONE _____

DDRESS _____ FAX _____

_____

AME _____ PHONE _____

DDRESS _____ FAX _____

_____

AME _____ PHONE _____

DDRESS _____ FAX _____

_____

AME _____ PHONE _____

DDRESS _____ FAX _____

NAME _____ PHONE _____

ADDRESS _____ FAX _____

_____

NAME _____ PHONE _____

ADDRESS _____ FAX _____

_____

NAME _____ PHONE _____

ADDRESS _____ FAX _____

_____

NAME _____ PHONE _____

ADDRESS _____ FAX _____

_____

NAME _____ PHONE _____

ADDRESS _____ FAX _____

_____

NAME _____ PHONE _____

ADDRESS _____ FAX _____

_____

NAME _____ PHONE _____

ADDRESS _____ FAX _____

NAME

ADDRESS

PHONE

FAX

NAME

ADDRESS

PHONE

FAX

NAME

ADDRESS

PHONE

FAX

NAME

ADDRESS

PHONE

FAX

NAME

ADDRESS

PHONE

FAX

NAME

ADDRESS

PHONE

FAX

NAME

ADDRESS

PHONE

FAX

NAME

PHONE

ADDRESS

FAX

NAME

PHONE

ADDRESS

FAX

NAME

PHONE

ADDRESS

FAX

NAME

PHONE

ADDRESS

FAX

NAME

PHONE

ADDRESS

FAX

NAME

PHONE

ADDRESS

FAX

NAME

PHONE

ADDRESS

FAX

Lighthouse, Blacksod Bay

For back to the past, though the thought brings woe,
My memory ever glides—
To the old, old, time, long, long ago,
The time of the Barmecides!
—James Clarence Mangan (1803–1849)
The Time of the Barmecides

County Kerry

Dews lay pearly
In the lily-bell and rose.
Up from each green leafy bosk and hollow
Rose the blackbird's pleasant lay,
And the soft cuckoo was sure to follow—
'Twas the Dawning of the Day.
—James Clarence Mangan (1803–1849)
The Dawning of the Day

NAME

ADDRESS

PHONE

FAX

NAME

ADDRESS

PHONE

FAX

NAME

ADDRESS

PHONE

FAX

NAME

ADDRESS

PHONE

FAX

NAME

ADDRESS

PHONE

FAX

NAME

ADDRESS

PHONE

FAX

NAME

ADDRESS

PHONE

FAX

NAME _____ PHONE _____

ADDRESS _____ FAX _____

_____

NAME _____ PHONE _____

ADDRESS _____ FAX _____

_____

NAME _____ PHONE _____

ADDRESS _____ FAX _____

_____

NAME _____ PHONE _____

ADDRESS _____ FAX _____

_____

NAME _____ PHONE _____

ADDRESS _____ FAX _____

_____

NAME _____ PHONE _____

ADDRESS _____ FAX _____

_____

NAME _____ PHONE _____

ADDRESS _____ FAX _____

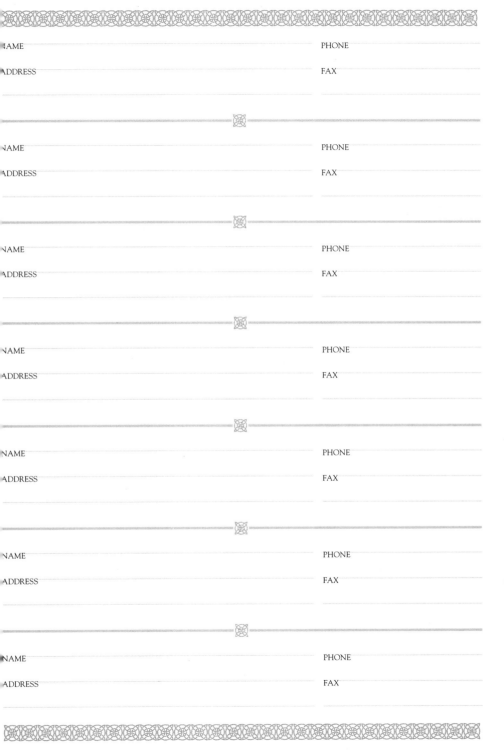

NAME

PHONE

ADDRESS

FAX

NAME

PHONE

ADDRESS

FAX

NAME

PHONE

ADDRESS

FAX

NAME

PHONE

ADDRESS

FAX

NAME

PHONE

ADDRESS

FAX

NAME

PHONE

ADDRESS

FAX

NAME

PHONE

ADDRESS

FAX

NAME _____ PHONE _____

ADDRESS _____ FAX _____

_____ _____

NAME _____ PHONE _____

ADDRESS _____ FAX _____

_____ _____

NAME _____ PHONE _____

ADDRESS _____ FAX _____

_____ _____

NAME _____ PHONE _____

ADDRESS _____ FAX _____

_____ _____

NAME _____ PHONE _____

ADDRESS _____ FAX _____

_____ _____

NAME _____ PHONE _____

ADDRESS _____ FAX _____

_____ _____

NAME _____ PHONE _____

ADDRESS _____ FAX _____

Ben Bulben, County Sligo

O the sunshine of old Ireland, when it lies
On her woods and on her waters;
And gleams through her soft skies,
Tenderly as the lovelight in her daughters' Gentle eyes.
—John Todhunter (1839–1916)
Longing

K

K

Thatched roofs, County Wexford

Each year the pleasant prospect shrinks,
And houses close the olden view;
The world is changing fast; he thinks
The sun himself is failing too.
—Thomas Caulfield Irwin (1823–1892)
A Character

NAME

PHONE

ADDRESS

FAX

NAME

PHONE

ADDRESS

FAX

NAME

PHONE

ADDRESS

FAX

NAME

PHONE

ADDRESS

FAX

NAME

PHONE

ADDRESS

FAX

NAME

PHONE

ADDRESS

FAX

NAME

PHONE

ADDRESS

FAX

NAME   PHONE

ADDRESS   FAX

NAME   PHONE

ADDRESS   FAX

NAME   PHONE

ADDRESS   FAX

NAME   PHONE

ADDRESS   FAX

NAME   PHONE

ADDRESS   FAX

NAME   PHONE

ADDRESS   FAX

NAME   PHONE

ADDRESS   FAX

NAME _____ PHONE _____

ADDRESS _____ FAX _____

_____

NAME _____ PHONE _____

ADDRESS _____ FAX _____

_____

NAME _____ PHONE _____

ADDRESS _____ FAX _____

_____

NAME _____ PHONE _____

ADDRESS _____ FAX _____

_____

NAME _____ PHONE _____

ADDRESS _____ FAX _____

_____

NAME _____ PHONE _____

ADDRESS _____ FAX _____

_____

NAME _____ PHONE _____

ADDRESS _____ FAX _____

NAME

PHONE

ADDRESS

FAX

NAME

PHONE

ADDRESS

FAX

NAME

PHONE

ADDRESS

FAX

NAME

PHONE

ADDRESS

FAX

NAME

PHONE

ADDRESS

FAX

NAME

PHONE

ADDRESS

FAX

NAME

PHONE

ADDRESS

FAX

Valentia, County Kerry

When the boys began to gather in the glen of a summer night,
And the Kerry piper's tuning made us long with wild delight,
O, to think of it; O, to dream of it, fills my heart with tears.
—James Lyman Molloy (1837–1909)
The Kerry Dance

L

Cliffs of Moher, County Clare

…An Amalthea's horn
Of rathe delight seemed emptied from on high
On all the progeny of land and sea—
Shore-maidens sang and sea birds shrieked for glee.
—John Todhunter (1839–1916)
Morning in the Bay of Naples

AME   PHONE

DDRESS   FAX

AME   PHONE

DDRESS   FAX

AME   PHONE

DDRESS   FAX

AME   PHONE

DDRESS   FAX

AME   PHONE

DDRESS   FAX

AME   PHONE

DDRESS   FAX

AME   PHONE

DDRESS   FAX

NAME

PHONE

ADDRESS

FAX

NAME

PHONE

ADDRESS

FAX

NAME

PHONE

ADDRESS

FAX

NAME

PHONE

ADDRESS

FAX

NAME

PHONE

ADDRESS

FAX

NAME

PHONE

ADDRESS

FAX

NAME

PHONE

ADDRESS

FAX

NAME

PHONE

ADDRESS

FAX

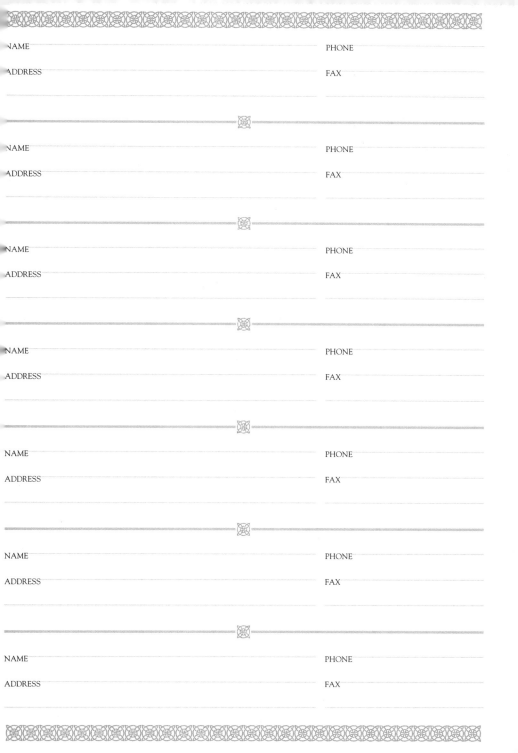

NAME

PHONE

ADDRESS

FAX

NAME

PHONE

ADDRESS

FAX

NAME

PHONE

ADDRESS

FAX

NAME

PHONE

ADDRESS

FAX

NAME

PHONE

ADDRESS

FAX

NAME

PHONE

ADDRESS

FAX

NAME   PHONE

ADDRESS   FAX

NAME   PHONE

ADDRESS   FAX

NAME   PHONE

ADDRESS   FAX

NAME   PHONE

ADDRESS   FAX

NAME   PHONE

ADDRESS   FAX

NAME   PHONE

ADDRESS   FAX

NAME   PHONE

ADDRESS   FAX

County Donegal

Sweet is a voice in the land of gold,
Sweet is the calling of wild birds bold;
Sweet is the shriek of the heron hoar,
Sweet fall the billows of Bundatrore.
—From the Irish: Oisin
Translated by George Sigerson
Things Delightful

County Galway

M

Each morn he basks away the hours
In garden nooks, and quaffs the air;
Chats with his plants, and holds with flowers
A tender-toned communion there;
—Thomas Caulfield Irwin (1823–1892)
A Character

NAME

PHONE

ADDRESS

FAX

NAME

PHONE

ADDRESS

FAX

NAME

PHONE

ADDRESS

FAX

NAME

PHONE

ADDRESS

FAX

NAME

PHONE

ADDRESS

FAX

NAME

PHONE

ADDRESS

FAX

NAME

PHONE

ADDRESS

FAX

NAME _____ PHONE _____

ADDRESS _____ FAX _____

_____

NAME _____ PHONE _____

ADDRESS _____ FAX _____

_____

NAME _____ PHONE _____

ADDRESS _____ FAX _____

_____

NAME _____ PHONE _____

ADDRESS _____ FAX _____

_____

NAME _____ PHONE _____

ADDRESS _____ FAX _____

_____

NAME _____ PHONE _____

ADDRESS _____ FAX _____

_____

NAME _____ PHONE _____

ADDRESS _____ FAX _____

NAME   PHONE

ADDRESS   FAX

NAME   PHONE

ADDRESS   FAX

NAME   PHONE

ADDRESS   FAX

NAME   PHONE

ADDRESS   FAX

NAME   PHONE

ADDRESS   FAX

NAME   PHONE

ADDRESS   FAX

NAME   PHONE

ADDRESS   FAX

NAME _____ PHONE _____

ADDRESS _____ FAX _____

_____

NAME _____ PHONE _____

ADDRESS _____ FAX _____

_____

NAME _____ PHONE _____

ADDRESS _____ FAX _____

_____

NAME _____ PHONE _____

ADDRESS _____ FAX _____

_____

NAME _____ PHONE _____

ADDRESS _____ FAX _____

_____

NAME _____ PHONE _____

ADDRESS _____ FAX _____

_____

NAME _____ PHONE _____

ADDRESS _____ FAX _____

County Mayo

Across the mountains all aglow,
Upon the lonely bridge we turned
To watch the roseate, russet hue,
Till faint and fainter still it burned
As if 'twere quenched by falling dew.
—Charles J. Kickam (1828–1882)
St. John's Eve

Bective Abbey, County Meath

The empty ruins, lapsed again
Into Nature's wide domain,
Sow themselves with seed and grain
As Day and Night and Day go by;
And hoard June's sun and April's rain.
—William Allingham (1824–1889)
The Ruined Chapel

NAME   PHONE

ADDRESS   FAX

NAME   PHONE

ADDRESS   FAX

NAME   PHONE

ADDRESS   FAX

NAME   PHONE

ADDRESS   FAX

NAME   PHONE

ADDRESS   FAX

NAME   PHONE

ADDRESS   FAX

NAME   PHONE

ADDRESS   FAX

NAME

PHONE

ADDRESS

FAX

NAME

PHONE

ADDRESS

FAX

NAME

PHONE

ADDRESS

FAX

NAME

PHONE

ADDRESS

FAX

NAME

PHONE

ADDRESS

FAX

NAME

PHONE

ADDRESS

FAX

NAME

PHONE

ADDRESS

FAX

NAME

ADDRESS

PHONE

FAX

NAME

ADDRESS

PHONE

FAX

NAME

ADDRESS

PHONE

FAX

NAME

ADDRESS

PHONE

FAX

NAME

ADDRESS

PHONE

FAX

NAME

ADDRESS

PHONE

FAX

NAME

ADDRESS

PHONE

FAX

NAME   PHONE

ADDRESS   FAX

NAME   PHONE

ADDRESS   FAX

NAME   PHONE

ADDRESS   FAX

NAME   PHONE

ADDRESS   FAX

NAME   PHONE

ADDRESS   FAX

NAME   PHONE

ADDRESS   FAX

NAME   PHONE

ADDRESS   FAX

County Kerry

Oh, Ireland is a pleasant place when youth is in the veins,
'Tis pleasant when the sun is out, 'tis pleasant when it rains.
Fore sure the eyes of youth can pierce the thickest rain or mist,
And see afar the mountains by the kindly sunshine kissed.
—Denis A. McCarthy (?–1931)
Going Back

O

✦ *Atlantic Coast*

O the springtime in old Ireland! O'er the sea
I can smell our hawthorn bushes,
And it all comes back to me—
The sweet air, the old place, the trees, the cows, the thrushes
Mad with glee.

—John Todhunter (1839–1916)
Longing

NAME   PHONE

ADDRESS   FAX

NAME   PHONE

ADDRESS   FAX

NAME   PHONE

ADDRESS   FAX

NAME   PHONE

ADDRESS   FAX

NAME   PHONE

ADDRESS   FAX

NAME   PHONE

ADDRESS   FAX

NAME   PHONE

ADDRESS   FAX

NAME   PHONE

ADDRESS   FAX

NAME   PHONE

ADDRESS   FAX

NAME   PHONE

ADDRESS   FAX

NAME   PHONE

ADDRESS   FAX

NAME   PHONE

ADDRESS   FAX

NAME   PHONE

ADDRESS   FAX

NAME   PHONE

ADDRESS   FAX

NAME   PHONE

ADDRESS   FAX

NAME   PHONE

ADDRESS   FAX

NAME   PHONE

ADDRESS   FAX

NAME   PHONE

ADDRESS   FAX

NAME   PHONE

ADDRESS   FAX

NAME   PHONE

ADDRESS   FAX

NAME   PHONE

ADDRESS   FAX

NAME

PHONE

ADDRESS

FAX

NAME

PHONE

ADDRESS

FAX

NAME

PHONE

ADDRESS

FAX

NAME

PHONE

ADDRESS

FAX

NAME

PHONE

ADDRESS

FAX

NAME

PHONE

ADDRESS

FAX

NAME

PHONE

ADDRESS

FAX

County Cork

P

A little sun, a little rain,
A soft wind blowing from the west,
And woods and fields are sweet again,
And warmth within the mountain's breast.
—Stopford Augustus Brooke (1832–1916)
The Earth and Man

P

Ferns, County Wexford

And glittering fanes, and lofty towers,
All on this fairy isle are seen:
And waving trees, and shady bowers,
With more than mortal verdure green.
—Luke Aylmer Conolly (?–c. 1833)
The Enchanted Island

NAME _____ PHONE _____

ADDRESS _____ FAX _____

_____

NAME _____ PHONE _____

ADDRESS _____ FAX _____

_____

NAME _____ PHONE _____

ADDRESS _____ FAX _____

_____

NAME _____ PHONE _____

ADDRESS _____ FAX _____

_____

NAME _____ PHONE _____

ADDRESS _____ FAX _____

_____

NAME _____ PHONE _____

ADDRESS _____ FAX _____

_____

NAME _____ PHONE _____

ADDRESS _____ FAX _____

NAME _____ PHONE _____

ADDRESS _____ FAX _____

_____ _____

NAME _____ PHONE _____

ADDRESS _____ FAX _____

_____ _____

NAME _____ PHONE _____

ADDRESS _____ FAX _____

_____ _____

NAME _____ PHONE _____

ADDRESS _____ FAX _____

_____ _____

NAME _____ PHONE _____

ADDRESS _____ FAX _____

_____ _____

NAME _____ PHONE _____

ADDRESS _____ FAX _____

_____ _____

NAME _____ PHONE _____

ADDRESS _____ FAX _____

_____ _____

NAME

ADDRESS

PHONE

FAX

NAME

ADDRESS

PHONE

FAX

NAME

ADDRESS

PHONE

FAX

NAME

ADDRESS

PHONE

FAX

NAME

ADDRESS

PHONE

FAX

NAME

ADDRESS

PHONE

FAX

NAME

ADDRESS

PHONE

FAX

NAME _____ PHONE _____

ADDRESS _____ FAX _____

_____

NAME _____ PHONE _____

ADDRESS _____ FAX _____

_____

NAME _____ PHONE _____

ADDRESS _____ FAX _____

_____

NAME _____ PHONE _____

ADDRESS _____ FAX _____

_____

NAME _____ PHONE _____

ADDRESS _____ FAX _____

_____

NAME _____ PHONE _____

ADDRESS _____ FAX _____

_____

NAME _____ PHONE _____

ADDRESS _____ FAX _____

West Cork

QR

We think how great had been our bliss,
If Heav'n had but assign'd us
To live and die in scenes like this,
With some we've left behind us!
—Thomas Moore (1779–1852)
As Slow Our Ship

QR

Valentia, County Kerry

There's honey in the leaf and the blossom,
And honey in the night and the day,
And honey-sweet the heart in Love's bosom,
And honey sweet the words Love will say.
—Katharine Tynan-Hinkson (1861–1931)
Summer-Sweet

NAME   PHONE

ADDRESS   FAX

NAME   PHONE

ADDRESS   FAX

NAME   PHONE

ADDRESS   FAX

NAME   PHONE

ADDRESS   FAX

NAME   PHONE

ADDRESS   FAX

NAME   PHONE

ADDRESS   FAX

NAME   PHONE

ADDRESS   FAX

NAME   PHONE

ADDRESS   FAX

NAME   PHONE

ADDRESS   FAX

NAME   PHONE

ADDRESS   FAX

NAME   PHONE

ADDRESS   FAX

NAME   PHONE

ADDRESS   FAX

NAME   PHONE

ADDRESS   FAX

NAME   PHONE

ADDRESS   FAX

NAME

ADDRESS

PHONE

FAX

NAME

ADDRESS

PHONE

FAX

NAME

ADDRESS

PHONE

FAX

NAME

ADDRESS

PHONE

FAX

NAME

ADDRESS

PHONE

FAX

NAME

ADDRESS

PHONE

FAX

NAME

ADDRESS

PHONE

FAX

NAME

PHONE

ADDRESS

FAX

NAME

PHONE

ADDRESS

FAX

NAME

PHONE

ADDRESS

FAX

NAME

PHONE

ADDRESS

FAX

NAME

PHONE

ADDRESS

FAX

NAME

PHONE

ADDRESS

FAX

NAME

PHONE

ADDRESS

FAX

County Laois

It seemed to whisper "Quietness,"
Then quietly itself was gone:
Yet echoes of its mute caress
Were with me as the years went on.

—A. E. (?), 1800s
The Three Counsellors

S

County Westmeath

Watching out for the hallowed shore,
All other attractions scornin':
O Ireland! don't you hear me shout?
I bid you the top o' the mornin'.
—John Locke (1847–1889)
The Exile's Return, or Morning on the Irish Coast

NAME _____   PHONE _____

ADDRESS _____   FAX _____

_____

NAME _____   PHONE _____

ADDRESS _____   FAX _____

_____

NAME _____   PHONE _____

ADDRESS _____   FAX _____

_____

NAME _____   PHONE _____

ADDRESS _____   FAX _____

_____

NAME _____   PHONE _____

ADDRESS _____   FAX _____

_____

NAME _____   PHONE _____

ADDRESS _____   FAX _____

_____

NAME _____   PHONE _____

ADDRESS _____   FAX _____

NAME

ADDRESS

PHONE

FAX

NAME

ADDRESS

PHONE

FAX

NAME

ADDRESS

PHONE

FAX

NAME

ADDRESS

PHONE

FAX

NAME

ADDRESS

PHONE

FAX

NAME

ADDRESS

PHONE

FAX

NAME

ADDRESS

PHONE

FAX

NAME

PHONE

ADDRESS

FAX

NAME

PHONE

ADDRESS

FAX

NAME

PHONE

ADDRESS

FAX

NAME

PHONE

ADDRESS

FAX

NAME

PHONE

ADDRESS

FAX

NAME

PHONE

ADDRESS

FAX

NAME

PHONE

ADDRESS

FAX

NAME _____ PHONE _____

ADDRESS _____ FAX _____

_____

NAME _____ PHONE _____

ADDRESS _____ FAX _____

_____

NAME _____ PHONE _____

ADDRESS _____ FAX _____

_____

NAME _____ PHONE _____

ADDRESS _____ FAX _____

_____

NAME _____ PHONE _____

ADDRESS _____ FAX _____

_____

NAME _____ PHONE _____

ADDRESS _____ FAX _____

_____

NAME _____ PHONE _____

ADDRESS _____ FAX _____

_____

County Wicklow

I'm weary for old Ireland—once again
To see her fields before me,
In sunshine or in rain!
And the longing in my heart when it comes o'er me
Stings like pain.

—John Todhunter (1839–1916)
Longing

T

Skelligs, County Kerry

I dreamt I reached the Irish shore and felt my heart rebound
From wall to wall within my breast, as I trod that holy ground....
—Thomas Darcy McGee (1825–1868)
To Duffy in Prison

T

NAME

ADDRESS

PHONE

FAX

NAME

ADDRESS

PHONE

FAX

NAME

ADDRESS

PHONE

FAX

NAME

ADDRESS

PHONE

FAX

NAME

ADDRESS

PHONE

FAX

NAME

ADDRESS

PHONE

FAX

NAME

ADDRESS

PHONE

FAX

NAME

ADDRESS

PHONE

FAX

NAME

ADDRESS

PHONE

FAX

NAME

ADDRESS

PHONE

FAX

NAME

ADDRESS

PHONE

FAX

NAME

ADDRESS

PHONE

FAX

NAME

ADDRESS

PHONE

FAX

NAME

ADDRESS

PHONE

FAX

NAME

ADDRESS

PHONE

FAX

NAME

ADDRESS

PHONE

FAX

NAME

ADDRESS

PHONE

FAX

NAME

ADDRESS

PHONE

FAX

NAME

ADDRESS

PHONE

FAX

NAME

ADDRESS

PHONE

FAX

NAME

ADDRESS

PHONE

FAX

NAME _____ PHONE _____

ADDRESS _____ FAX _____

_____ _____

NAME _____ PHONE _____

ADDRESS _____ FAX _____

_____ _____

NAME _____ PHONE _____

ADDRESS _____ FAX _____

_____ _____

NAME _____ PHONE _____

ADDRESS _____ FAX _____

_____ _____

NAME _____ PHONE _____

ADDRESS _____ FAX _____

_____ _____

NAME _____ PHONE _____

ADDRESS _____ FAX _____

_____ _____

NAME _____ PHONE _____

ADDRESS _____ FAX _____

_____ _____

River Boyne, County Meath

And I long for the dear old river,
Where I dreamed my youth away;
For a dreamer lives forever,
And a toiler dies in a day.
—John Boyle O'Reilly (1844–1890)
The Cry of the Dreamer

Galbally, County Limerick

If you would like to see the height of hospitality,
The cream of kindly welcome, and the core of cordiality:
Joys of all the olden time—you're wishing to recall again?
Come down to Donovans, and there you'll meet them all again.
—Francis A. Fahy (1854–?)

UV

NAME _____ PHONE _____

ADDRESS _____ FAX _____

_____

NAME _____ PHONE _____

ADDRESS _____ FAX _____

_____

NAME _____ PHONE _____

ADDRESS _____ FAX _____

_____

NAME _____ PHONE _____

ADDRESS _____ FAX _____

_____

NAME _____ PHONE _____

ADDRESS _____ FAX _____

_____

NAME _____ PHONE _____

ADDRESS _____ FAX _____

_____

NAME _____ PHONE _____

ADDRESS _____ FAX _____

NAME   PHONE

ADDRESS   FAX

NAME   PHONE

ADDRESS   FAX

NAME   PHONE

ADDRESS   FAX

NAME   PHONE

ADDRESS   FAX

NAME   PHONE

ADDRESS   FAX

NAME   PHONE

ADDRESS   FAX

NAME   PHONE

ADDRESS   FAX

NAME _____ PHONE _____

ADDRESS _____ FAX _____

_____

NAME _____ PHONE _____

ADDRESS _____ FAX _____

NAME _____ PHONE _____

ADDRESS _____ FAX _____

NAME _____ PHONE _____

ADDRESS _____ FAX _____

NAME _____ PHONE _____

ADDRESS _____ FAX _____

NAME _____ PHONE _____

ADDRESS _____ FAX _____

NAME _____ PHONE _____

ADDRESS _____ FAX _____

NAME _____

PHONE _____

ADDRESS _____

FAX _____

_____

NAME _____

PHONE _____

ADDRESS _____

FAX _____

_____

NAME _____

PHONE _____

ADDRESS _____

FAX _____

_____

NAME _____

PHONE _____

ADDRESS _____

FAX _____

_____

NAME _____

PHONE _____

ADDRESS _____

FAX _____

_____

NAME _____

PHONE _____

ADDRESS _____

FAX _____

_____

NAME _____

PHONE _____

ADDRESS _____

FAX _____

_____

Lough Easky, County Sligo

A shadow of cloud on the stream
Changes minute by minute....
—William Butler Yeats (1865–1939)
Easter 1916

W

West Cork

On this I ponder, where'er I wander,
And thus grow fonder, sweet Cork, of thee....
—Francis Sylvester Mahony ("Father Prout") (1804–1866)
The Bells of Shandon

W

NAME   PHONE

ADDRESS   FAX

NAME   PHONE

ADDRESS   FAX

NAME   PHONE

ADDRESS   FAX

NAME   PHONE

ADDRESS   FAX

NAME   PHONE

ADDRESS   FAX

NAME   PHONE

ADDRESS   FAX

NAME   PHONE

ADDRESS   FAX

NAME _____ PHONE _____

ADDRESS _____ FAX _____

_____ _____

NAME _____ PHONE _____

ADDRESS _____ FAX _____

_____ _____

NAME _____ PHONE _____

ADDRESS _____ FAX _____

_____ _____

NAME _____ PHONE _____

ADDRESS _____ FAX _____

_____ _____

NAME _____ PHONE _____

ADDRESS _____ FAX _____

_____ _____

NAME _____ PHONE _____

ADDRESS _____ FAX _____

_____ _____

NAME _____ PHONE _____

ADDRESS _____ FAX _____

NAME   PHONE

ADDRESS   FAX

NAME   PHONE

ADDRESS   FAX

NAME   PHONE

ADDRESS   FAX

NAME   PHONE

ADDRESS   FAX

NAME   PHONE

ADDRESS   FAX

NAME   PHONE

ADDRESS   FAX

NAME   PHONE

ADDRESS   FAX

NAME

ADDRESS

PHONE

FAX

NAME

ADDRESS

PHONE

FAX

NAME

ADDRESS

PHONE

FAX

NAME

ADDRESS

PHONE

FAX

NAME

ADDRESS

PHONE

FAX

NAME

ADDRESS

PHONE

FAX

NAME

ADDRESS

PHONE

FAX

Gortahinty, Shannon, County Leitrim

And this I dare avow,
there are more rivers, lakes, brooks,
strands, quagmires,
bogs, and marshes in this country
than in all Christendom besides.

—William Lithgow (1582–1645)

 Ferry Carrick, County Wexford

Not every thought can find its words,
Not all within is known;
For minds and hearts have many chords
That never yeld their tone....
—W. E. H. Lecky (1838–1903)
Undeveloped Lives

NAME

PHONE

ADDRESS

FAX

NAME

PHONE

ADDRESS

FAX

NAME

PHONE

ADDRESS

FAX

NAME

PHONE

ADDRESS

FAX

NAME

PHONE

ADDRESS

FAX

NAME

PHONE

ADDRESS

FAX

NAME

PHONE

ADDRESS

FAX

NAME _____ PHONE _____

ADDRESS _____ FAX _____

_____

NAME _____ PHONE _____

ADDRESS _____ FAX _____

_____

NAME _____ PHONE _____

ADDRESS _____ FAX _____

_____

NAME _____ PHONE _____

ADDRESS _____ FAX _____

_____

NAME _____ PHONE _____

ADDRESS _____ FAX _____

_____

NAME _____ PHONE _____

ADDRESS _____ FAX _____

_____

NAME _____ PHONE _____

ADDRESS _____ FAX _____

NAME   PHONE

ADDRESS   FAX

NAME   PHONE

ADDRESS   FAX

NAME   PHONE

ADDRESS   FAX

NAME   PHONE

ADDRESS   FAX

NAME   PHONE

ADDRESS   FAX

NAME   PHONE

ADDRESS   FAX

NAME   PHONE

ADDRESS   FAX

NAME

PHONE

ADDRESS

FAX

NAME

PHONE

ADDRESS

FAX

NAME

PHONE

ADDRESS

FAX

NAME

PHONE

ADDRESS

FAX

NAME

PHONE

ADDRESS

FAX

NAME

PHONE

ADDRESS

FAX

NAME

PHONE

ADDRESS

FAX